"For anyone who has conscientiously sought to nurture trust-based relationships in their professional life only to be perplexed as to why such are successful in some cases and frustrating in others, this fable offers clear diagnosis and renewed hope, with a few chuckles and a hearty laugh or two. A delightful and actionable read!"

—Stephen Mangum, Senior Associate Dean, Professor of Management and Human Resources, Fisher College of Business, The Ohio State University

"In *A Slice of Trust*, Hutchens and Rellaford dish up a simple yet powerful serving that can help to make a real difference in an organization. By applying Smart Trust, presented here so clearly and with humor, your organization can reap the rewards of *A Slice of Trust*."

—Claudio Morelli, Superintendent of Schools, Burnaby Board of Education, Burnaby, B.C., Canada

"*A Slice of Trust* is a delightful and entertaining story packed with invaluable truths and wisdom about the importance of trust in effective leadership. Its message will transform your thinking about the key role trust plays in personal, professional and organizational success."

—Greg Tillar, CEO, NuGrowth Solutions

"*A Slice of Trust* is a fun and fast read that illustrates the payoff of extending trust wisely, and the painful tendency most of us have to make it more complicated than necessary. Don't miss this!"

—Jim Brown, author of *The Imperfect Board Member* and Consulting Partner, STRIVE!

"A must-read that reinforces why work can be so rewarding! Trust amplifies and accelerates all aspects of the business. The smart trust we extend to each other, combined with the belief of what we can do together in the future, fuels an incredible environment for individuals who value innovation, teamwork and results!"

—Pamela Springer, President & CEO, Manta

"*A Slice of Trust* is served with warmth and humor. Pour yourself a cup of tea and enjoy a few bites of wisdom for the workplace."

—Mette Norgaard, author of *The Ugly Duckling Goes to Work*

"Brilliantly written allegory that teaches the nuances and business value of trust!"

—Lisa Wardle, Managing Director, Duke Corporate Education

A Slice

of

TRUST

The Leadership Secret
with the *Hot & Fruity* Filling

David Hutchens & Barry Rellaford
Foreword by Stephen M.R. Covey

GIBBS SMITH
TO ENRICH AND INSPIRE HUMANKIND

First Edition
15 14 13 12 11   5 4 3 2 1

Published by
Gibbs Smith
P.O. Box 667
Layton, Utah 84041

1.800.835.4993 orders
www.gibbs-smith.com

Designed by Debra McQuiston
Printed and bound in Hong Kong

Gibbs Smith books are printed on either recycled, 100% post-consumer waste, FSC-
certified papers or on paper produced from sustainable PEFC-certified forest/controlled
wood source. Learn more at www.pefc.org.

Library of Congress Cataloging-in-Publication Data

Hutchens, David, 1967–
  A slice of trust : the leadership secret with the hot & fruity filling / David Hutchens &
Barry Rellaford ; foreword by Stephen M. R. Covey. — 1st ed.
      p. cm.
  ISBN 978-1-4236-2118-8
  1. Business ethics. 2. Trust. 3. Success in business. I. Rellaford, Barry. II. Title.
  HF5387.H864 2011
  658.4001'9—dc22
                              2010043165

Contents

Foreword

by Stephen M. R. Covey,
Author, *The Speed of Trust*

I'll never forget an experience several years ago when our company had been working with two distinct suppliers to provide the same product for our business. On paper, the suppliers looked similar. Both had good people and reputations. We started off trusting them both. But while one supplier consistently performed, the other one didn't. Our trust in the one grew and in the other shrank. We had to put in place redundant inspection processes for the supplier that was inconsistent, which cost us extra time and money, causing our product costs to rise. We ultimately decided to drop that supplier and just go with the one we trusted.

After this experience, I found myself noticing everywhere the same phenomenon: that the *economic* implications of trust were as great as, if not greater than, the *social* implications. I ran with this simple insight and began to see the impact of trust—or the lack thereof—everywhere. I found that when I consciously focused on trusting and being trusted, it brought great success—and when trust was neglected or ignored, I paid the price. I eventually concluded that *trust is the one thing that changes everything,* and today I am only more convinced that is true. This conviction, along with empirical data and a personal sense of passion for this topic, led to the development and publication of my book, *The Speed of Trust: The One Thing that Changes Everything.*

Because trust is such a simple idea, it is typically underestimated, assumed and taken for granted. It seems we only appreciate it after we lose it. Yet this oft-neglected subject of trust has yielded untold layers of depth as our company has explored its many uses and applications among individuals, teams, organizations, and society. Most fascinating, even with all the work we've done in dozens of countries, I believe we've only just scratched the surface. There is much more work to do, and that's what excites me most. That is why I am so pleased to have on my team practitioners like Barry Rellaford and David Hutchens, who help our trust approach come to life. Barry has served as one of the chief architects and global advocates for our approach, while David has developed learning tools and products that even today are helping our practice lead a transformation of trust all around the world.

These authors understand trust. Barry, more than anyone, helped me shape and mold the ideas and terms in *The Speed of Trust*. He has been a constant supporter and expert advisor for the work we're doing. Most significantly, he has been an insightful coach and facilitator in working with client organizations throughout the world, particularly with executive teams, in teaching and helping them implement the Speed of Trust on their teams and in their organizations in order to achieve sustained superior performance.

David, in turn, has paid the price to master our content, which, coupled with his innate gifts of writing and storytelling, has given him the ability to convey key messages in a way that is both simple and profound. He understands how people and organizations learn, and he's created tools and processes to enable and accelerate that learning. The combination of Barry and David in producing this wonderful book is an illustration of the speed of trust in action!

When they first approached me about this project, I must admit I was a bit skeptical. I'm typically not a big fan of fables—many of them aren't very well told or the stories often get in the way of the message or they come across as naively simplistic. But because I trusted the authors, I agreed to read their story and was delightfully surprised. As well as I know the topic of trust and what we've learned together in taking this message to individuals and organizations everywhere, I was still captivated by the characters and flow of the narrative —and laughed as I read about Simon's and Sebastian's choices and the consequences of the subsequent actions. Every time I found myself worrying about the message possibly missing an important idea, the authors had anticipated that very point, which would soon manifest itself as the story continued in greater depth. I was pleased—and impressed.

A Slice of Trust depicts the purposeful balance of choice, analysis, emotion, judgment and personal courage required for exercising trust. As you join Simon the Pieman on his adventures in trust, I invite you to reflect on how you have extended trust in your organization, your relationships, your family, your world. After all, the most important story is *your* story. It's a story that you create every day as you explore opportunities for trust. And it's a story whose telling is brought to life every time you extend your trust to another, one slice at a time.

So, welcome to this conversation on trust down a different— yet parallel—path from *The Speed of Trust*. As you experience the *Speed* of Trust in your world, we'd like to hear from you. Tell us your challenges in practicing "Smart Trust." Let us know where your journey is taking you and how we might help you take the next step. Along the way, I am confident that you will discover, as I have, that nothing is as fast as, more inspiring than, more satisfying than, or more filling than a simple slice of trust.

—Stephen M. R. Covey
March 2011

CHAPTER 1

In Which a Pieman Adopts an Unusual Business Strategy

Simon the old Pieman was gone,
and the village mourned.

Old Sebastian mourned too.

For years he had been Simon's business partner, and co-owner of Simon's Pie Shoppe.

When Sebastian announced that Simon Jr. would step up to take his father's place, villagers gasped.

"Surely you don't mean young Simon? *Simple* Simon?"

"Yes, yes," Sebastian explained patiently. "'Twas his father's wish."

"But he doesn't know pastries. Not like his father!"

"Aye, but he does," Sebastian defended. "When he was but a wee lad, he helped to roll out the crusts for his father and me."

"But Simon the younger cannot possibly run a business."

For this, Sebastian had no response. He stared down at his flour-dusted boots and muttered, "We shall see."

"Bonjour, Sebastian!" called out a cheery young Simon early the next morning as he stepped into the shop and fired up the old brick oven.

Sebastian eyed Simon closely as his nimble fingers went to work mixing the blueberries, rolling the dough, and shaping the ingredients into perfect little round pies.

To be sure, he has his father's talent, Sebastian thought.

But people say this young man is naive. They say he is too trusting.

By mid-morning, a wisp of smoke curled from the little stone chimney, filling the village square with a sweet, buttery aroma. Just as it always had.

Located right on the village square, just across from the blacksmith, and in between a guillotine store called The Cutting Edge and a new boutique called Leeches! Etc., the shop had been the only place to go for the sweetest, most buttery fruit-filled pies for more than forty years.

And just as his father had always done, Simon opened the windows of the shop and looked out on the street before him.

"*Tarte chaude!*"[1] he called and waved to passersby from the window of his little store. "Get your *tarte chaude!*"

The villagers looked at one another, and raised an eyebrow. Many had the same thought: *He sounds just like his father.*

---

1. This is French for "hot pie."

Just as they had for the decades before, the irresistible smells drew a small crowd of milkmaids, highwaymen, villains and knaves, the poor, the privileged, and even a couple of venture capitalists to his open window.

"A slice of blackberry, *pour la jolie jeune fille*?"[2] Simon called as Colette, the merry milkmaid, passed.

"Aye, Simon," Colette said as she took a slice and bit into it.

"Why, Simon! These are every bit as good as your father's," she purred, showing her blueberry-stained teeth. "I'll have another please."

"*Bon appétit!*"[3]

---

2. This is French for "the pretty young lady."
3. This is French for "Bon appetit."

When she left, Sebastian growled; "Simon, she did not pay for that slice of pie."

"*Oui*, but Colette, she is a good friend."

Sebastian snorted. "Simon, we run a business, not a charity."

Indeed, in the years before the death of Simon the Wise, the pie shop had struggled. Investor over-speculation had driven blackberry markets sky-high, and the current village administration was applying pressure to break the country's dependence on foreign cooking oil.

Simon the Wise and Sebastian had even discussed plans to close the shop, but that was just before Simon the Wise had fallen ill. "We shall decide later," the elder Simon had said at the time. But they never did.

Sebastian squinted at Simon and shook his head sadly.

'Twas a fine, brilliant June morning, and the little village square was already teeming with commerce.

Indeed, it was the biggest sales day of the year, for it was the date of the annual trade show for local peasants and unwashed masses, which this year had been advertised with the theme *Synergy: 1600 AD.*

Like the year before, the little pie shop was positioned in the high-traffic area just outside of the tent for the big keynote address (which in the trade show program was listed as Six Sigma, Process Improvement, and Manure: Reducing Waste in Waste.)

"*Ooh la la!* We make *beaucoup de tartes chaudes!*" Simon said to Sebastian.

"Aye," he said, not sharing Simon's merry tone. "We have been making pies all night. We will cover our expenses today if we can handle the crowds."

The sun was soon high in the sky, and the afternoon keynote had come to an end. Hungry trade show attendees streamed from the tent and quickly formed a long line at the window of the little shop.

"One slice of blueberry pie, kind sir," said the old lady at the front of the line.

Simon called, "*Oui! Une partie de la tartie!*"[4]

"What did he just say?" the old lady asked Sebastian, for she was unable to see the footnote.

"'One slice of pie,'" Sebastian translated. "That'll be two pence, ma'am."

And so it went. Simon shuttled pies from the pie shelf, to the big clay oven, to the cutting board, and then to the window while Sebastian collected money and counted out the change.

---

4. Roughly translated as "one slice of pie." Please do not check our French on this.

The line grew longer. Supplies—and patience—quickly grew short.

"Hey, what's the holdup?" called customers from the back of the line.

"More pies! For the love of St. Crisco, more pies!" called Sebastian from his position at the window, but the poor harried pie man couldn't keep up.

Sebastian and Simon both watched as several customers became frustrated and left for one of those new McHaggis stores that were popping up all over the place.

Sebastian and Simon shot a worried glance at each other: *We're losing business.*

That's when Simon called out to the line of hungry customers: "It is okay. You make the change!"

"Excuse me?" Sebastian whispered to the simple pie man where the customers could not hear him. "What are you talking about?"

"We make *les tartes*. Let them make the change!" Simon placed a small mixing bowl on the window ledge, next to the fresh slices. He dropped a few coins into the bowl.

"Simon!" said Sebastian, trying to comprehend. "Surely you're not saying we should leave the window and the money bowl unattended! Why, 'twould be foolish to trust these people! Do you not know that this village is full of villains and knaves?"

"Come, come," Simon insisted, as he tugged Sebastian gently away from the window.

The customer at the window watched all of this with surprise. "So, you wish for me to serve myself and count out my own change?"

"*Mais oui!*" said Simon. "Go ahead! We trust you. We'll be in the back making more *tartes chaudes*."

"This is madness!" Sebastian protested in a fierce whisper as Simon guided him toward the pie-assembly table at the back of the shop.

"How much for a slice?" the puzzled customer called.

"Read the sign!" Simon called back from the back of the shop.

The customer read aloud, "*No public restrooms*."

"Other sign!"

The customer read aloud, "*One slice / Two pence*."

The customer shrugged, took one slice of blackberry pie, and dropped a five-pence coin into the bowl.

Then he reached his hand into the bowl and counted out his change: one, two, three pence.

"G'day, Simon!" he called, and the next customer quickly advanced in the line. That customer took two slices of blueberry and dropped exact change—four pence—into the bowl and then quickly moved away.

"Sebastian, come! We make *plus de tartes*!"[5] Nervously, Sebastian turned to the ovens with Simon and began crafting more pies, while the customers continued to serve themselves and drop money into the mixing bowl.

For the rest of the afternoon, Sebastian and Simon left the pie window unattended and instead worked together to make more pies. Customers approached the window and helped themselves, dropping money into the bowl. Some were incredulous, but most expressed delight at the arrangement.

The line moved more quickly than it ever had before.

And the two men, working together, made more pies than they ever had before.

---

5. "More pie." Come on. You should have been able to figure that one out on your own.

But the stress was giving Sebastian a tension headache, for working at the piecrust table meant turning his back to the window, the bowl, and the money.

'Tis irresponsible, that's what it is, thought Sebastian, and he wondered what Simon the Wise, rest his soul, would say if he knew the old crust baker had abdicated his post as money counter.

The sun was setting and shadows grew long as the last of the customers sauntered away from the dusk-hued village square. Sebastian could hardly wait to get to the money—if, in fact, those knaves had not taken it all!

A wave of relief swept over Sebastian when he took the bowl and saw that it did, indeed, contain a mound of coins.

Just as he did every evening at closing, Sebastian opened his special leather-bound edition FranklinCovey Pie Ledger. He counted the leftover slices, and then tallied up the sold inventory:

28 blueberry: 52 pence
21 blackberry: 39 pence
                  91 pence

Hmmm. Not bad at all! he thought.

But then he squinted harder at the numbers. *Wait a minute, something is afoul!* Sebastian thought. He scribbled a few calculations and scratched his beard. Yes, the numbers were off. The 28 blueberry slices *should* have earned 56 pence, *not* 52; the 21 blackberry, 42, *not* 39.

Sebastian scribbled a few more numbers. Seven pence were unaccounted for. An 8 percent loss!

Sebastian's cheeks burned bright red. *I knew it!* he hissed through clenched teeth. *We have been robbed!*

Was this because customers were fools who counted out their change incorrectly?

Or was this a result of knaves and thieves who brazenly stole a few coins from the change bowl?

It was hard to say *why* the money was missing. But one thing was for sure: *Simon's experiment in trust had made fools of them.*

This would be the end for Simon's Pie Shoppe.

"Young Simon," Sebastian said sadly, shaking his head, "your papa was a proud man, and he would be proud of your trusting heart. But I made him a promise that I would watch out for you and the pie shop, and I must tell you, when dealing with fools and knaves, one must be careful with his trust."

"*Non!*" Simon exclaimed. "Not a failure! The customers, they are *bon*."

"Simon," Sebastian said in a steady voice as he maintained direct eye contact, "you need to understand: we suffered an 8 percent loss today."

"*Non!* Not a loss!" Simon flipped back through the pages of the Pie Ledger. He found the numbers for last year's convention crowd and pointed emphatically. "Look!"

Sebastian looked, and compared them to this year's numbers:

Year 1600

28 blueberry:	52 pence
21 blackberry:	39 pence
	91 pence

Year 1599

11 blueberry:	22 pence
13 blackberry:	26 pence
	48 pence

"By the beard of Saint Canola, you're right, Simon!" Sebastian said. "We brought in 43 pence more than last year!" Sebastian rubbed his belly as he studied the numbers. "By trusting customers to make their own change, everything moved faster."

"*Oui! Plus de tartes chaudes!*" Simon said, delighted.

"That's right," Sebastian agreed. "More pies. And also more speed, more efficiency . . . more money."

"*Onh, honh, honh!*"[6] Simon snorted, and did a little jig.

---

6. We have no idea what this means. Must be a French thing.

But that night in his darkened cottage, Sebastian tossed and turned, unable to sleep.

The shop's pies sales were 43 pence more than the previous year. The gain was significant.

Perhaps his partner, the simple pie man, was on to something.

But was it worth it? *To be sure, we sold more pie. But we lost seven pence to knaves and villains,* he thought. Sebastian did not like to be made a fool.

Sebastian rose from his bed, lit a candle, and dipped a feather quill into his ink jar. He sketched in his journal:

Extending Trust:

risk, loss   speed, efficiency

So is it wise to trust . . . or not? he thought.

It was late in the night before he could fall asleep.

That night, while Simon, Sebastian, and the rest of the village slept, a light burned in the little shop just across the square from Simon's.

Cows in the nearby stables mooed in protest as a cloaked figure hammered a nail into the old wooden door of the building, and hung a hand-painted sign.

Then the cloaked figure slipped away into the fog, and the night was quiet again.

CHAPTER 2

The Fruits of Trust

The next morning, Simon arrived at the pie shop, whistling a happy tune, and was surprised to find Sebastian already there, his face as pale as lard.

"Simon, did you see?"

"*Non*," Simon said, puzzled. "*Qu'est-ce que c'est?*"[7]

"Look!" Sebastian pointed out the window to the little shop, which up until now had stood vacant right next door to the Malaria & Plague Quick Clinic (Walk-Ins Welcome)."

The new sign read:

"That . . . that *knave!*" Sebastian stuttered. "He has copied our business model! I wouldn't be surprised if he stole our recipes as well! Our market cannot bear another pie shop. He wants to steal our customers, like some sort of pied piper. This shall be our end, Simon."

Simon simply and calmly said, "Come. We have work."

---

7. "What is this?" (No, we're not asking you what this is. We're trying to tell you that's the translation of qu'est-ce que c'est. Oh, never mind.)

As the sun rose, customers lined up at Simon's Pie Shoppe.

The trade show crowds from earlier in the week had left town, but, amazingly, the line was almost the same length it had been during those peak sales days. Perhaps the townspeople had heard the buzz about the strange little shop that trusted people to serve themselves and count their own change.

All day long, one after another, customers came to the window, served themselves, dropped money into the bowl, and counted out their change.

Most of them smiled, waved, and shouted their thanks to Simon, who was hard at work at the back of the store.

Of course, Sebastian kept a watchful eye on Pies by Igor just across the square, which appeared to do brisk business throughout much of the day. Every time a new customer walked to Igor's window, Sebastian felt his heart sink just a little as he wondered: *Now that Igor has copied our business, what do we have that makes us different?*

In fact, Sebastian was standing at the window watching Igor's shop, and just happened to look down as one of Simon's customers took two slices of blueberry, dropped a five pence in the bowl, and walked away.

"Sir!" Sebastian called to the customer. "You forgot to take your change!"

"No, sir, I didn't!" the man called back and waved. "You can keep the change!"

That evening as Simon prepared to close the shop, Sebastian reviewed the day's transactions:

23 blueberry   49 pence
20 blackberry: 41 pence
                                      90 pence

"Simon, would you come look at this?"

Simon studied the numbers with Sebastian. "*Tres bien*."

"Yes, it is," Sebastian agreed. "Did you notice that the numbers don't add up?"

"*Oui.*"

"We should have taken in 86 pence from today's sales. But we made 90."

"*Oui.*"

"A few customers *over*paid for their pie."

"*Oui.*"

"And I don't think it was a mistake," Sebastian said. "I watched at least one customer leave his change on purpose."

"*Oui*," said Simon, who acted as if this were the most natural thing in the world.

Sebastian just stood there with his hand on his chin, staring at the numbers. "Incredible."

That evening when he returned home from work, Sebastian opened his journal, dipped a feather quill into ink, and wrote:

Being trusted invites people to be their best

Then Sebastian thought about the shop's new capability for serving many more slices of pie in the same amount of time. It was Simon's trust that had made this increase possible.

He wrote:

Trust = Speed

Sebastian blew out the candle and went to the window to draw the curtains, but he saw something that made him pause: a shadowy figure was emerging from Igor's shop.

He looked closely as the figure pulled back its hooded cloak in the moonlight and turned toward a streetlamp.

It was Colette, the milkmaid.

What kind of dealings could she possibly have with Igor?

He felt a familiar burn of suspicion in his chest.

Simon was not going to like this.

CHAPTER 3
Into the Marketplace

The next morning, Simon loaded 20 fresh slices of pie and placed them onto a wooden cart.

The cart had a crudely painted sign on one side that said "Simon's Pies." On the other side, Simon had written: "Put money in bowl. Count your own change."

Simon had placed a wooden bowl on the cart and was just about to wheel the cart out the front door when Sebastian arrived.

"Good morning, Simon," he said. "Where are you taking those pies?"

"To Le Stock Market."[8]

"Are you crazy?" Sebastian said, eyeing the little hand-painted sign. "That's three blocks away. You're *leaving* the pies there? This is not wise! It is true that yesterday most of your customers behaved honorably. But this is different!

"At our shop window, customers could *see* us," Sebastian continued. "They *knew* they could get caught stealing. But if you leave your pies unattended three blocks away, where is the accountability? This is not trust. This is madness!"

---

8. No, not that kind of stock market. This is home of Giuseppe Soprano's handmade chains, stocks, straitjackets, and other gifts for the dungeon keeper in your life. Giuseppe saves you money by eliminating the middle man! (And yes, he actually eliminates the middle man.)

Simon just stared at Sebastian with a smile fixed on his face. "Sebastian, stay here and make *les tartes chaudes*. Simon says!"

Aargh, Sebastian thought. *He exercised the "Simon Says Clause." Now I have to comply. It's right there in my contract.*

Simon left for the Stock Market while Sebastian went to his workstation in silence.

When Simon returned to the shop a short time later, Sebastian was waiting there, tapping his foot.

"Simon, I have been patient," he said. "But you have gone mad. You shall make fools of us, if you do not destroy your father's business first. Why, even your *petite fille* Colette has betrayed your trust. That's right. She is now working for Igor!"

Simon's cheeks flushed, and he looked away and held up his hand. "Do not speak of that," Simon said solemnly, and Sebastian suddenly felt ashamed of himself.

After a few moments of silence, Simon only said, quietly, "Let's sell some pie."

It was another day of strong sales and delighted customers.

As afternoon approached, Simon left the pie shop to retrieve the cart from the Stock Market, three blocks away.

He returned fifteen minutes later.

The cart was empty.

"We sold all twenty!" he announced to Sebastian, and held up a burlap bag that jingled with metal coins.

Sebastian took the bag of coins and quickly emptied it onto the table. He began arranging the coins in little stacks. *Two pence . . . four pence . . . six pence . . . eight . . .*

He counted until he placed the last coin at the top of a stack.

Total: 39 pence. A loss of only a single pence.

And now Simon's Pie Shoppe had a whole new channel for selling pie that appeared to be nearly limitless.

"Simon, you are a titan of business!" Sebastian exclaimed.

"*Non*," Simon said. "I just trust wisely."

Simon stepped to a cabinet at the back of his shop. He reached high to the top shelf and pulled down a small, flat item that was wrapped in plain brown paper.

"*Pour toi*," Simon said, as he handed the mysterious package to Sebastian.

"What is it?"

"A gift. My father, he gave it to me. I know he would want you to have it."

That night, alone in his little hut at the edge of the village, Sebastian's thoughts raced.

Perhaps his friend, simple Simon, wasn't so simple at all. He was growing the business, and really, all he had done was extend trust to the people around him.

It seemed simple. Almost too simple. It couldn't be *that* easy—could it?

Sebastian unwrapped the gift that Simon had given him. As the paper wrapping fell away, it revealed a piece of old, yellowed fabric, under glass and held in place by a gilded frame.

On the fabric was a hand-embroidered message:

TO TRUST IS TO LEAD

This was a new idea to Sebastian. It had never occurred to him that the two ideas might be so closely connected.

Sebastian thought, *if it is so simple, why is it so hard for ME to extend trust? Why does it seem so natural for Simon? Do some people just have a higher tendency to trust?*

I always thought it was irresponsible to trust people.

But just look at Simon's results. Who is the irresponsible one?

He looked at the embroidered gift sitting next to his bed and was still for a long time.

Suddenly Sebastian knew what he wanted to do.

CHAPTER 4

Sebastian's Trust Experiment

The next morning, Sebastian was first to arrive at the pie shop. As a beam of sunlight streamed through the window of the store, Sebastian loaded 40 fresh slices of pie onto the wooden cart.

"Sebastian!" Simon called, just as Sebastian was about to wheel the pies away. "What is this?"[9]

"Good morning, Simon! Your propensity to trust others has been an inspiration, my friend, and today I too shall extend my trust!"

"And where are you taking *ces tartes*?"

"To the Dark Forest!" Sebastian said.

Simon's smile quickly left his lips.

---

9. In French, this would be "Que est-ce que c'est?" Be thankful Simon said it in English this time, because these tiresome translation footnotes are wearing out their welcome.

"Here's my idea," Sebastian said. "Your experiment with the cart worked brilliantly. Now we shall take it even further. I will place pie carts all across the forest and collect the money at the end of the day.

"Just think—" Sebastian continued, his eyes wide with excitement, "lots of people live in that forest, and the more we extend trust, the more money we will make! Now the only limit to our success is our capacity to make pies. It's brilliant, Simon!"

But Simon shook his head. "*Non*. I do not like."

"Trust me, Simon," said Sebastian.

Simon looked at his old friend. "Aye, I trust *you*," he said, but as Sebastian stepped outside the shop, Simon's eyes were sad.

"Now, how will I get this old pie cart to the Dark Forest?" Sebastian wondered out loud, for the path to the forest was rocky and the cart was quite heavy, with big wooden wheels hewn from timber.

Tied to a post just outside of the shop were Millie and Matilda—the pie shop's two oxen.

"Which one of you girls should I trust with my precious cargo?" he asked the two animals aloud. Both oxen grunted in response.

Sebastian deliberated as he looked at Matilda, then to Millie, then back to Matilda again. Millie had labored for Sebastian for years. Yes, the old girl's legs tended to wobble when work was strenuous. But she was genial and responsive to commands. Sebastian knew her well.

Matilda was a new ox, only recently acquired. She seemed to have a sour disposition, and Sebastian had no idea how well she would respond to his direction on the journey. But Matilda was certainly much stronger than Millie.

After a few moments of deliberation, he placed the yoke around the muscular neck of the young, untested Matilda. Leaving old Millie behind, he led the young ox and the cart full of pies out of town and toward the dark forest commonly known as the Dark Forest.

As he walked into the shadows of the Dark Forest with Matilda, Sebastian thought about the choice he had just made.

That was another decision about trust, it occurred to him as Matilda snorted. *I trust both oxen. But I trust them in very different ways.*

He decided this would be a good thing to keep thinking about.

His thoughts quickly turned from oxen back to pie and the profits he hoped to collect from the Dark Forest.

It was almost noon when Sebastian returned to the pie shop. He had left the cart in the dark forest and returned Matilda to her post outside the shop alongside Millie.

Customers were lining up at the little shop window to serve themselves, so Sebastian quickly joined Simon, who was already hard at work making pies.

The day passed quickly—and profitably.

The hour became late, the sky burned orange and red, and it was time to retrieve the profits from the Dark Forest.

Simon volunteered to make the journey while Sebastian stayed behind to clean up.

It was dark, and Sebastian was wiping flour from the crust table by candlelight when Simon at last came through the front door. Simon's head was hanging low.

"Simon!" Sebastian said happily. "How much money did we make in the Dark Forest?"

"*Zéro*," Simon said. "They took the money."

"What?" Sebastian felt his heart race. "You mean there was nothing at all in the bowl?"

"They took the bowl."

"So I guess they also took all the slices from the cart as well," he said.

"They took the cart."

Sebastian was stunned.

Sebastian could hardly find the words to speak. "I . . . don't understand, Simon," he said. "I trusted them! When you trust people, they're supposed to respond by being trustworthy."

Perhaps *trust* was a foolish leadership strategy after all.

"*Non*," Simon said. "In the Dark Forest, they do not know me. They do not know my father. So they take *les tartes*."

"I knew it!" Sebastian said through clenched teeth. "People are not to be trusted! I shall never trust again!"

"*Non*. Do not lose your trust in yourself, *mon ami*. For when you lose trust in self, you lose *all* trust."

Simon continued, "You must practice *la confiance lucide*."

"'*Smart trust*?'" Sebastian asked. His thoughts were racing, and his chest felt tight.

"*Oui*. It is work."

"Sebastian, I have another gift I wish to give to you. It is from my father."

Simon handed Sebastian another small wrapped package. Beneath the brown paper he could feel the edges of another frame.

"Another one?" Sebastian said. "So I'm guessing you have quite a few of these little embroidered axioms?"

"*Mais oui*! My father, he was fascinated with stitched wisdom. He made *beaucoup*. Towards the end, the quality was, how do you say, not so good. His last one just said "Check Your Zipper.""

"But this one, I know you will like."

Sebastian unwrapped the brown paper. The framed cloth read:

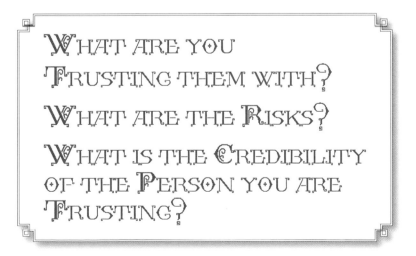

WHAT ARE YOU
TRUSTING THEM WITH?
WHAT ARE THE RISKS?
WHAT IS THE CREDIBILITY
OF THE PERSON YOU ARE
TRUSTING?

Wow, that is an unusually specific embroidered message, Sebastian thought. *But those do seem like good questions to think about when extending Smart Trust.*

"It is clear that you have extended your trust to *me*," Sebastian said, sadly. "And I have failed you. I have much to think about."

'Twas the middle of the night and Sebastian was once again wide awake.[10] He played the events of the past several days over and over in his mind:

Simon trusted the customers at the window; they responded with trust.

Simon trusted the employees at The Stock Market; they also responded with trust.

Then I trusted the people of the Dark Forest. They took advantage of my trust.

Something changed. But what?

Sebastian wasn't sure. But clearly, it was not always wise to extend trust.

---

10. You must remember, dear reader, that this was before the age of doctor-prescribed sleep medications and that in the old days, anxious people had little recourse but to stare at the ceiling. And yes, we know, we said we were through adding footnotes but this one was really important.

He wrote:

> *All trust is not the same.*
>
> *Some trust is wise.*
>
> *Some Trust is foolish.*

It seemed there was quite a difference between the smart trust that Simon had practiced and Sebastian's trust, which had been so foolish.

But what was it?

"Simon had discernment," Sebastian finally said out loud.

Simon had carefully considered his decision to trust, while Sebastian had rushed into the Dark Forest without weighing the risks. Simon the Wise had captured it well in his embroidered maxims.

Smart Trust made all of the difference.

Sebastian thought about this for a few moments. Surely it is not a *bad* thing to be suspicious, especially in a time such as this, where villains and knaves were all about. In fact, he was certain that in the past his distrust had secured the pie shop against loss.

But, clearly, it also prevented a lot of opportunity.

Simon, on the other hand, had chosen a different path—one that was fraught with risk and rich with reward. He had cho sen to trust.

And now Simon was reaping the rewards of his smart trust— and, of course, his delicious pie.

Simon dipped his quill into the ink once more. He wrote:

Trust is built over time, one slice at a time.

"Simon, I wish to ask you a question," Sebastian said the next morning as they were opening the shop.

"Ask," he said.

"Yesterday, before I left for the Dark Forest, you told me you trusted me."

"*Oui*," he said.

"But you knew I was making a mistake."

"*Oui.*"

"I was doing something *stupide* that was going to hurt the business, although I'm sure you would never use those words."

"Yes, I would. It was stupid."

"I am confused," Sebastian said. "How is that smart trust?"

"Hmm," Simon thought. "That reminds me of a gift I have for you." He pulled a small item wrapped in brown paper from the shelf.

Another one? Good grief, why even go to the trouble of wrapping these things? Sebastian thought.

He unwrapped it.

NEVER DRINK
ORANGE JUICE
RIGHT AFTER
BRUSHING YOUR
TEETH

"Pardon," Simon said. *"Excusez-moi.* Wrong one. Open this one."

He handed another package to Sebastian, who rolled his eyes and unwrapped it.

TRUST in:
WHO THEY ARE
WHAT THEY
CAN DO

"Two different kinds of trust," Sebastian observed.

"*Oui*. Both are good. Both *together* is best."

Sebastian immediately thought of Millie and Matilda. He had chosen the stronger ox for the job, despite her sour temperament, because he trusted in her ability to get the work done.

But it was not an ideal choice. Simon was right—it is best to have both kinds of trust together.

"So, you trusted who I am, right?" said Sebastian, thinking through this difference between character and competence.

"*Oui*. I knew your intent."

"Even though you did not believe in what I was doing."

"*Oui*, but I was willing to lose 40 pies so you could see that many times we learn more from our mistakes than our successes."

Sebastian thought for a moment. "So you weighed the risks of losing the pies against the opportunities of having me learn about extending trust. That was *smart trust*."

"*Oui*."

It was all coming together now. It was remarkable, really, how many factors this simple pie man had apparently considered before extending smart trust: "the risk of lost sales and inventory; the desire people have to be trusted (and their tendency to respond by being trustworthy); the opportunity to build capacity in others, and the regard the villagers had for Simon's family name.

Simon had even weighed Sebastian's own character in relation to his ability.

Thinking aloud, Sebastian said:

> ## "The work of trust is hard.
> ## The risks are real.
> ## The reward is high."

"*Tres bien!*" Simon said, reflecting on Sebastian's thoughts. And then he added: "You should embroider that!"

"Excuse me, sir!" a customer called from the window, interrupting them. "Are you open for business?"

A line had formed, and it was longer than ever.

"*Oui!*" Simon called back. "Serve yourself! You make the change!"

Sebastian and Simon glanced at one another. Simon winked. "Let's go bake *les tartes*," he said to his old friend.

Another Slice

One fine morning, Simon was polishing the new limestone-and-granite baking table that he had just purchased for the shop. It was a fine, sturdy table with ample workspace—and a daily reminder of the growing business and the rewards of trust.

There was a knock at the door.

"*Qui est la?* Who is there?"

"Hello, Simon." It was Colette, the milkmaid. She stood at the window, looking down nervously.

"Colette, *ma cherie*! What are you doing here?" Then he added, "I heard that you have been working for Igor."

"Yes," she said sheepishly. "I wish to work for *you*."

Simon went to the window and looked about. No one else was around.

He looked directly at Colette and listened expectantly.

Colette's bottom lip trembled as she struggled to hold back tears. At last she spoke.

"I no longer wish to work for Igor," she confided. "He watches every little move his workers make. He does not trust. He has people who double check all the work, so it takes us twice as long as it should."

Simon just listened and nodded.

"One never knows whether Igor is happy with them. The other workers, they betray one another just so they can impress Igor. But they have lost their passion for the work. People quit all the time.

"And . . . and . . ." Colette paused to compose herself, but a tear streamed down her cheek.

"And . . . " she continued at last, "his ingredients for his pie are not good. He uses filler ingredients to save money but does not tell his customers."

"*Zut alors!*" Simon said.

She leaned forward and whispered, "*He uses blackbirds.*"

"*Excusez-moi?*"

"Yes, blackbirds. He bakes them into his pie."

Simon's eyes were wide with horror. "How many?"

"A lot. Four and twenty."

"Four and twenty blackbirds!?"

"Four and twenty blackbirds. Baked in a pie."

Simon could hardly comprehend this breach of public trust.

"Everyone knows it is different here at your shop," Colette said, wiping her tears. "I wish to be a part of something greater. I do not know a lot about how you bake your pies, but I work hard, and I can learn."

Simon looked at Colette with compassion. He liked her spirit.

He opened the door and motioned for her to come in. "Have a seat, *mon amie*," he said, as he pulled up a padded stool.

Then he smiled and said,
"May I offer you a slice of pie?"

La Fin[11]

---

11. The End

MORE SLICES OF TRUST

A Look at
La Confiance Lucide

by Barry Rellaford

I'm going to take a wild guess here, and assume that you are *not* in the business of pie.

That's okay. Because at the end of the workday, it doesn't matter whether your fingertips are stained with ink, engine oil, or blueberries, because, like Simon the Pieman, each of us engages in countless interactions with other human beings every day. And each of these transactions—whether you are addressing a conflict, discussing how to do the work, or offering someone a fruity pastry—is accompanied by a choice: *how* will I engage with this person? What kind of precedent am I establishing in this single interaction? How will this affect my ability to get work done in the future?

And even more fundamentally, *am I increasing or decreasing trust with this interaction?*

A few years ago, Stephen M. R. Covey called me to get some help regarding a conference where he had been asked to deliver an important presentation. The conference organizers wanted him to send his slides in advance. I asked him, "Do you need help with PowerPoint?" He said, "I don't have a speech!"

I asked Stephen what the topic was. "It's called the *Speed* of Trust," he said.

This idea resonated with me instantly and deeply. Trust is something I've thought of and cared about a lot over the years. It's been at the heart of my career journey, and at the core of the great relationships I enjoy.

As we worked together to develop that first speech, I found that while Stephen didn't have slides, he did have a lifetime of invaluable insight and experience in the area of trust.

The more we talked, the more difficult it became to imagine any kind of interaction that was not quantitatively and qualitatively impacted by trust. As we shared the evolution of our thoughts with our clients, colleagues, and loved ones, we were struck by the urgency that everyone seemed to feel when it came to the subject of trust. One senior financial officer confided in us, "You guys nailed it. Trust is *the* issue. I deal with it daily."

This was unusual. A lot of the work I do is considered "soft." I help people work together effectively, deliver better results within teams, and discover their purpose. It all seems "lovey dovey Covey" to some. And yet we were meeting very experienced line executives and financial stewards—people who live and die by the "hard" business capabilities—clamoring to know more about this soft topic. It really got our attention.

Then we entered the worst global economic storm in generations. The creation, maintenance, loss, or reestablishment of trust became, for many of these leaders, the most strategically sensitive item on their corporate agendas.

So what about you? What brings you to this conversation? Have you enjoyed the strength of relationship that comes with strong trust? Have you wondered *who* you can trust— and *with what* and *when* and *why*? Have you experienced the sheer efficiency and *speed* that is possible in your work when people trust each other?

Or have you perhaps experienced the weary existence of being in a low-trust organization or relationship?

Either way, welcome to the conversation. He may be a simple pieman from some vaguely medieval age, but "simple" Simon has something profound to say that is deeply relevant to modern organizations.

We've generated a series of questions that you can consider, either by yourself or, even better, with people in your life where trust matters—the people you work or live with. You may want to note your own responses and ideas in a journal and decide which ones you want to act on to earn the dividends of trust.

Let's spend a few moments taking a closer look at *the one thing that changes everything.*

Discussion 1
Talk about this:

• Why do you think there is renewed interest in the topic of trust in organizations? Why are so many people thinking about this now?

• What are some other changes in the marketplace (or in our world and society) that are making trust more important than ever?

• What do you bring to this conversation? Do you feel any personal urgency around the topic of trust? Why or why not?

Take a moment and think of someone you trust. What is it about that person that you trust?

Don't answer too quickly. Reflect on this a little bit. You will likely realize that trust is not absolute.

For example, when I have an important decision to make in my life, there's an older friend I always confide in. We met many years ago and he's been a mentor to me for my entire adult life. I listen carefully when he gives me counsel about really important things. I completely trust his character and judgment.

Just a few months ago, I began experiencing a sharp pain in one of my teeth. Of course, I didn't call my esteemed friend to figure out what was wrong. Instead, I went to see our family's dentist of the past eleven years. He quickly determined that I was royalty and outfitted me with a crown. I trust his expertise, and he fixed the problem quickly and for a fair price, just as I knew he would.

I've never asked my wise mentor for dental help, and I've never asked my dentist for important life counsel. The trust I have for each of them—though strong—is not interchangeable.

Sebastian made a similar observation when choosing between the two oxen, Millie and Matilda. Remember when he said, "I trust both . . . but I trust them in very different ways"?

Sebastian was getting to an important awareness about the *dimensionality* of trust. That is, trust is the product of both *character* ("who I am") and *competence* ("what I can do").

When most people think of trust, they usually think of the character piece first. Equally important, however, is competence. *Being* good and *doing* good are the two sides of the trust coin, and your credibility and influence rest on how well you display both. These are the essence of generating trust, and if we are to begin the important work of building trust in our organization or family, we have no choice but to begin at these very personal levels.

Discussion 2
Talk about this:

• Think of a time when you trusted someone's *character* but not their *competence*. How did that affect your ability to work together?

• Now think of a time when you trusted someone's *competence*, but not their *character*. What was that work relationship like?

• Which is the greater source of *your* credibility in your organization? If you were to compromise trust, would it more likely be due to your character or your competence? What are some steps you could take to begin creating balance between the two?

A decade ago, I think it may have been a little more difficult to engage busy business leaders around the topic of organizational trust. (After all, it's "soft," right?) Not anymore. Today the headlines continue to announce that we are in a "crisis of trust." Our faith in corporations, financial systems, government, religious and social institutions, and more has been shaken to its core.

Why should organizations talk about trust? The unanimous response from scores of organizational leaders is simple and direct: *because low trust is expensive!* In his best-selling book *The Speed of Trust,* Stephen M. R. Covey demonstrates that organizations with low trust experience a "trust tax" that results in tremendous losses to speed and profitability.

What are the taxes of a low-trust organization? They are *redundancy, bureaucracy, politics, disengagement, turnover, churn* (that is, constantly losing customers, stakeholders, employees, and projects and having to replace them with new ones), and even *fraud*.

In the story you just read, Colette painted a grim picture of the work culture at Igor's. But other than the business about the "four and twenty blackbirds," I've been in a lot of organizations where I could have used the very same language to describe what was going on. Haven't you? The losses in speed and energy are enormous. Like Colette, I chose to remove myself from those organizations, taking my energy, talent, ideas, passion, and consumer dollars elsewhere.

In contrast to the taxes of the low-trust organization, Stephen M. R. paints a very different picture of an organization that is high in trust. These organizations enjoy *dividends* that produce tremendous speed and efficiency. These dividends include *increased value, accelerated growth, enhanced innovation, improved collaboration, stronger partnering, better execution*, and *heightened loyalty*.

Today, billions of dollars are on the line. Early in the story, Sebastian asked, "What do we have that makes us different?" In an age of parity in products and services, trust represents one of the last—and most powerful—areas of differentiation. And, increasingly, it is becoming a critical organizational capability that is demanded by customers and stakeholders.

Discussion 3
Talk about this:

• Review the seven taxes of a low-trust organization (*redundancy, bureaucracy, politics, disengagement, turnover, churn, fraud*). Which of these have you experienced in your career? Share some examples.

• Now review the seven dividends of a high-trust organization (*increased value, accelerated growth, enhanced innovation, improved collaboration, stronger partnering, better execution, heightened loyalty*). Which of these is most important to improve or increase in your organization? Share some examples of how this would improve your ability to accomplish your job and fulfill your organization's mission.

I'm going to assume that since you are still reading you would like to leave behind the taxes of a low-trust organization and, like Simon, begin to experience the speed, innovation, collaboration, loyalty and growth of a high-trust organization.

Does this mean your organization should take a page from Simon's playbook, abandon its accounts receivable systems, and instead trust customers to leave their payments in a bowl?

Whether you pursue that specific strategy is up to you, but let's think it through as Simon did. One thing we can know with certainty is something that Simon displayed over and over again: that trust is built not by saying the right things but by *doing* something and *behaving* in ways that build trust.

In a book on the subject of trust, it would be tempting to conclude that *extending trust* is always the correct answer. Otherwise, you're no different from Igor. Right?

Wrong. The correct answer is not to always extend trust, but to *extend trust in the right way*.

It's an idea we call Smart Trust.

Really, the heart of *A Slice of Trust* is Sebastian's journey in coming to terms with this important idea.

Sebastian was on the right track to understanding *Smart Trust* when he wondered if some people just have a higher inclination to trust. Yes, some people do. We might imagine this as a scale that is your *propensity to trust*.

Propensity to trust is your willingness or tendency to trust people or organizations. It's situational, and it's based on your experience.

Where would you place yourself on this vertical scale? If you have a high propensity to trust, you extend trust easily and willingly. If you have a low propensity, you are not a bad person; it's just that you (like Sebastian) have had past experiences that increase your likelihood to hold back trust.

High Propensity

Low Propensity

Next, with a little prompting by some unlikely embroidered messages, Sebastian reflected that *discernment and analysis* were important to exercise when extending trust. This too can be rendered as a scale.

If you have *low analysis,* you haven't yet developed the skill or experience to consider the possible risks and/or the person or organization you're trusting. If you have *high analysis,* you apply thoughtful consideration before choosing whether to extend trust.

High Propensity

Low Analysis —————+————— High Analysis

Low Propensity

More specifically, analysis means considering *what* you're trusting someone with. (A few slices from your pie inventory, or an entire cartful?)

It means considering the risks involved. (Place the change bowl in your window, or leave it unattended in an unmonitored location?)

And, finally, it means analyzing the credibility (character and competence) of the person or organization to which you're extending trust. (Based on the information you have, are you more inclined to form a partnership with Colette or with Igor?)

So this combination of "analysis" and "propensity" results in one of those lovely four-quadrant models that we organizational practitioners use so much. This one illuminates some important ways of thinking about *la confiance lucide—Smart Trust*—in organizations.

Let's explore this model a little deeper. In the upper left quadrant, we begin with *blind trust*.

Blind Trust is where we begin our lives as infants and sometimes our careers. Here we have a high propensity or willingness to trust but haven't developed the skills or experience to wisely discern when to extend trust, or to whom. Practiced into adulthood, this creates problems and exacts trust taxes.

In our story, blind trust is illustrated by Sebastian's decision to leave the pie cart unattended in the Dark Forest. In our lives, it's manifested by our trusting that people will always do the right thing, keep their commitments, or choose to benefit others as well as themselves. Unfortunately, our life experience, like Sebastian's, tends to teach us otherwise. Sebastian erred not because he extended trust but because he did so blindly, without considering what he was trusting or whom. He failed to adequately calculate and plan for the risks, and the result was a painful tax on the little pie organization.

Do you know people who operate out of *blind trust*? I do. They tend to be happy, kind-hearted people—and more than a little naive. Extending blind trust can deliver good results if you're fortunate to come across people who are trustworthy. But if you come across people who lack character or competence? Ouch.

Most of us don't operate in Blind Trust, at least not all of the time. Let's look at the next quadrant to the lower left, which is *low propensity* accompanied by *low analysis*. This is the quadrant of *No Trust*.

High Propensity

BLIND TRUST

Low Analysis ——————— High Analysis

NO TRUST

Low Propensity

Think of someone you know who doesn't analyze the risks of trust, and simply doesn't extend trust. These are people who have *no* trust and tend to lack confidence or trust in anyone, including themselves. That's a tough spot to operate from. Most people in organizations can't afford to spend a lot of time here. If you, or others you work with do, you'll see indecision, lack of initiative, and people waiting to be told what to do. You stay out of trouble, usually, but you'll never grow and the organization will never benefit from your talent and passion. The long-term consequence, or trust tax, of working from this quadrant is a fundamental loss of contribution and confidence—in yourself, in your organization, and from your stakeholders.

We see this in the story where Colette lost confidence or trust in Igor (and perhaps in herself) to the point where she left to join the competition. She took her talent and contribution elsewhere.

The next one—lower right quadrant—is one to be wary of.

High Propensity

BLIND TRUST

Low Analysis ———————— High Analysis

NO TRUST   DISTRUST

Low Propensity

People who have low propensity or willingness to trust coupled with strong analysis skills exhibit *distrust*. In other words, they don't trust easily, and they can give you specific, carefully thought-out reasons why! Perhaps it began with trusting someone early in their career or life and being severely disappointed or betrayed. Whatever the seed, the full-grown fruit of *distrust* is unhealthy.

This quadrant tends to exact heavy trust taxes. Have you ever worked with or for someone who fundamentally didn't trust others? They tend to micromanage, "snoopervise," and wring and wear out your energy. Reporting to a manager in this quadrant can tax our self-confidence and drive us into the quadrant of *No Trust*. Of course, people who operate in this quadrant are confident they are making the only "smart" choice. But it's not always the "wise" choice.

Much of the story is really about Sebastian's struggle with his own distrust, which appeared reasonable and even prudent to him. Like most of us, Sebastian probably had enough life experience to convince him that this was the only way to operate. Its foundation, however, is *fear*. And fear is the opposite of leadership. It will never invite our or others' best work.

This brings us around the plus sign to the only place where we earn trust dividends: the quadrant of *Smart Trust*.

High Propensity

BLIND | SMART
TRUST | TRUST

Low Analysis ——————+—————— High Analysis

NO | DISTRUST
TRUST |

Low Propensity

When we exercise *Smart Trust*, we operate with a *high propensity* to trust—and we temper it with *high analysis*. We use both our heads and our hearts. We consider what we are entrusting and to whom while at the same time actively looking for opportunities to extend trust for the benefit of others and ourselves. Remember that compelling list of *trust dividends* that bring speed and opportunity to some organizations? This is the only zone that delivers them. It is the place where we have the confidence and trust in ourselves to be creative, innovate, collaborative, and take smart risks.

Of course, Simon is the hero of our story and our exemplar of *Smart Trust*. He may be a simple pieman, but he possesses confidence in himself and others. He wisely believes in people and balances that with his judgment of knowing who he can trust, and with what.

Look at his dramatic results and then ask yourself whether you believe that kind of growth and opportunity is possible in your organization.

With *Smart Trust*, it certainly is.

So if the benefits are so compelling, why don't people operate out of *Smart Trust* all of the time?

This is a difficult idea for some, especially for those who can provide ample justification for their *distrust*. Others think they are exercising leadership when they're really operating from *blind trust* and exposing themselves and their organizations to unwise risks.

For most people, the paths of least resistance are *blind trust* (trust everyone!) or *distrust* (trust only yourself!) But the easy paths are never the ones that deliver rewards, and *Smart Trust* is a path that requires choice and purposeful action. Yes, you will encounter losses. You won't always have things work out the way you want.

Yet you'll develop greater confidence and achieve better results from yourself and others. And you'll be able to accelerate your actions in dramatic ways.

Discussion 4
Talk about this:

• Are there some situations in which *distrust* is the legitimate choice?

• Are there some situations in which *blind trust* or *no trust* are legitimate choices?

• Think of examples of times you took action in each of the four quadrants. What happened? What were the results?

• Think of a time when you exercised *Smart Trust*, and were nonetheless disappointed. Does this mean *Smart Trust* isn't "worth it?" How does that experience affect your willingness to invest in *Smart Trust* in the future?

So, dear reader, where will you go from here? What will you do to begin extending *Smart Trust* in your organization?

Here are a few ideas for taking action right away:

• Remember what Sebastian noted in his journal: "To trust is to lead." Write this on a sticky note and put in on your computer or in your locker or on the dashboard of your car. (If you have the necessary skills you could cross-stitch it yourself.)

• Read *The Speed of Trust: The One Thing That Changes Everything,* by *Stephen M. R. Covey with Rebecca R. Merrill* (Free Press, 2006). There you will encounter the ideas from this book in much more detail. You'll learn more about the *waves of trust* that can extend from your behaviors out to the team, the organization, and the marketplace. You'll also explore the 13 behaviors for building trust (of which "extending *Smart Trust*" is only one).

• Share what you've learned from reading this story with your team or other key stakeholders in your organization. Get copies of this book and share it with members of your team so you can all learn to extend *Smart Trust* together and discuss the questions in this end piece.

• Go to *www.SpeedOfTrust.com* for more learning resources and next steps.

• Quickly assess your trust level by finding the "Got Trust" app on Facebook. Invite your Facebook friends to give you trust feedback!

• Participate in a Speed of Trust course at your workplace or at one of our public workshops. This experience will give you a deeper understanding and, more importantly, multiple opportunities to practice the skills of extending *Smart Trust*.

• Extend *Smart Trust* to someone. Think of some important work you need to get done. Consider both the character and competence of that person or organization. Clarify what you expect from them and make sure you know what they expect. Practice accountability and give them the support they need.

The story ended with the offer of a slice of pie from Simon to Colette. Likewise, your journey of trust begins not with grand pronouncements but with simple transactions; individual actions that you take, extending from your character and competence.

Look around you. Someone in your world is ready to help unleash speed, innovation, and opportunity. All they need is to be inspired and energized with your trust.

Will you take the risk?

APPENDIX 1
Sebastian's Journal

Extending Trust:

risk, loss   speed, efficiency

Being trusted invites people
to be their best

Trust = Speed

All trust is not the same.
Some trust is wise.
Some trust is foolish.

Trust is built over time,
one slice at a time.

APPENDIX 2
The Embroidered Wisdom
of Simon the Wise

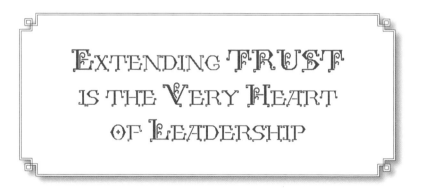

EXTENDING TRUST
IS THE VERY HEART
OF LEADERSHIP

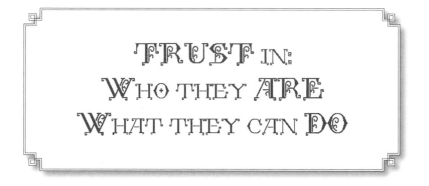

TRUST IN:
WHO THEY ARE
WHAT THEY CAN DO

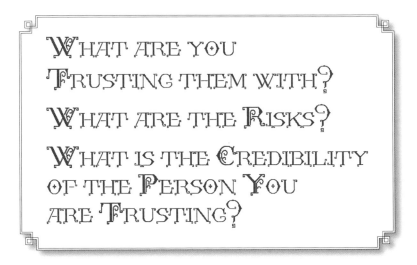

WHAT ARE YOU
TRUSTING THEM WITH?

WHAT ARE THE RISKS?

WHAT IS THE CREDIBILITY
OF THE PERSON YOU
ARE TRUSTING?

Wisdom from the later years. (The era of waning quality):

THAT HORIZONTAL-STRIPED SHIRT
MAKES YOU LOOK FAT

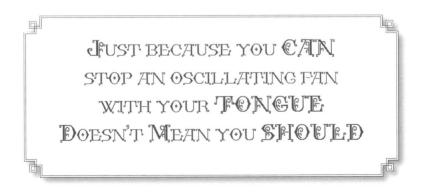

JUST BECAUSE YOU CAN
STOP AN OSCILLATING FAN
WITH YOUR TONGUE
DOESN'T MEAN YOU SHOULD

Acknowledgments

From David The act of writing a story is itself a story; a journey full of tests, surprise twists, and a gang of antagonists that most often are internal. The journey of creating this book is a story about heroes, and I'm indebted to the brave warriors who wielded swords, red editing pens, and a few slices of pie.

Don't tell Simon I told you, but his pies have a secret ingredient and her name is Donna Burnette. A trusted colleague for well over a decade, Donna has been one of my most trusted mentors in this vocation of organizational learning. I can't explain it: when Donna's around, things just seem to work, and when she's not, they don't. Thanks, Donna, for setting this process in motion.

Imagine you are Stephen M.R. Covey, Greg Link or anyone at the Franklin-Covey Global Speed of Trust Practice who has bet his future on the subject of organizational trust. Now imagine a couple of guys who say they want to pair that groundbreaking work with pie jokes. Stephen wasn't kidding in the foreword. This was an act of trust for him, and that only increases the value of his gift to us. Thank you, Stephen, and thank you, Greg.

Robbie is my best friend, which is why I married her, and she makes all of the trust stuff into a daily living lesson. It's okay if you didn't laugh at the funny parts in this book because Robbie did, and that's the only reaction I'm ever really going for. My two kids, Emory and Ollie, are like a couple of blue-berries in one of Simon's pies: so sweet you don't mind that they get a little sticky. Thank you for bringing the laughter.

And now we come to Barry Rellaford. How does one acknowledge such a prescient coach, gifted investor in people, and passionate maker of meaning? There are only five words that can express my admiration and appreciation: *ohn hohn hohn hohn hohn!*

From Barry I too am grateful to Donna for bringing the two of us together. It's a testament to trust that David and I didn't meet face-to-face until we were well through the manuscript and in the editing stage. The Donna Burnette trust bridge invited this reality.

David Hutchens is truly a partner—he listens well, gives beautiful voice to roughly framed ideas, and has a gentle sense of humor. David makes it safe to be true.

Publishing my writing in book form has been a lifelong call that I've had on hold until now. The call first came through Mr. Kim Ellison's English 10 class at Paradise High School in California. The assignment to turn in two pages of journaling a week has promoted a lifetime practice and one of my greatest experiences in a trusted mentor extending trust. (Not sure how smart it was, but it's made a profound difference!)

I'm grateful to my partners at CoveyLink, now the FranklinCovey Speed of Trust Practice—Stephen M. R. Covey, Greg Link, and Gary Judd—for their friendship and trust, and to the rest of our team, who are all committed to increasing trust in the world.

Family is one of the most powerful words and ideas I know—and I'm blessed with a wonderful one. Many thanks to Lorilee and our children— Matthew, Mark, Daniel, Greg, David, and Rebecca—who sacrifice their husband and Dad at times so I can be out sharing the message of extending smart trust.

My deepest acknowledgment is to my Creator—He has helped me learn to truly trust others and myself.

From Both of Us

The people of Gibbs Smith are uncommonly creative and collaborative publishers who chose to extend their trust to us. Thank you, Christopher Robbins and Madge Baird, for professionalism and creativity and for living the trust principles we describe in this book.

Other guides emerged on this hero's journey. Among them are Jessica McKenzie, a friend and kindred spirit who not only speaks the language of story but also has a crucial business sensitivity that seems to elude so many artists; David Kasperson and Marshall Snedaker of the Global Speed of Trust Practice, who bring endless energy, imagination, and fun to this project; Rowan Barnes-Murphy for his cool illustrations; and also Jedi story master Wendy Gourley, a partner of Katherine Farmer. With Katherine's StoryCone model, they just might have cracked the story code, and Wendy's application of that model as an analytic device to improve this story's structure was a small act of genius. Ladies, we do believe you are on to something.

—David Hutchens
—Barry Rellaford

About the Authors

David Hutchens has made a career of delivering big ideas to broad audiences in compelling ways.

He is creator and author of The Learning Fables—a series of books published by Pegasus Communications (Waltham, MA). The globally popular series includes the titles *Shadows of the Neanderthal, The Lemming Dilemma, Listening to the Volcano* and the perennial favorite *Outlearning the Wolves.* The unique combination of clever stories, sound business theory, and delightful illustrations have made the books a hit in corporate boardrooms, MBA programs, and even among groups of schoolchildren. The Learning Fables have sold more than 200,000 copies and have been published in more than a dozen languages.

A former award-winning advertising copywriter, David now works with some of the most influential organizations in the world to create change, learning and opportunity. As a writer, he has created communications solutions for The Coca-Cola Company, General Electric, and more. Also an executive speechwriter, he counts a CEO of The Coca-Cola Company among his clients.

Working with his partners in learning, he has created groundbreaking learning solutions for IBM, Walmart, Sam's Club, The Coca-Cola Company, Eli Lilly, Merck, Nike, BellSouth, and Booz Allen Hamilton.

David developed *The Speed of Trust Simulation,* an engaging discovery learning experience that is co-branded with Stephen M.R. Covey and based on his best-selling book, *The Speed of Trust.* He also developed *The Speed of Trust Meeting in a Box.*

David's programs have been recognized with distinctions such as ASTD's Excellence in Practice award, and HR Magazine's Training Product of the Year.

David lives just outside of Nashville, Tennessee, with his wife, Robbie, a Licensed Marriage and Family Therapist. Together they founded and operate Signet House LLC, a counseling center that serves the middle Tennessee area. They have two children, Emory and Ollie. They all like pie.

www.DavidHutchens.com

Barry Rellaford's great work is to help people discover, express, and fulfill *their* great work. His vocation of investing in people began in his youth in Paradise, California. From high school (where he engaged the student body as varsity mascot), through his undergraduate degree in Human Resource Development, and on to a master's degree from Ohio State's business school, Barry continued to engage and enlighten everyone he encountered.

Through his career, Barry has continually validated his teacher's prophetic assessment that he "plays well with others." As an influencer within Franklin-Covey, Barry led the Learning Expedition Center, the company's internal corporate university focused on the development of FranklinCovey salespeople and consultants. He also served as the Vice President of Organizational Development for Metatec Corporation and as a performance consultant at CompuServe Inc.

Barry is a co-founder of CoveyLink, the predecessor to FranklinCovey's Global *Speed of Trust* practice. Today he balances his trust work with his own practice, GreatWork, where he inspires individuals and organizations to perform meaningful and purposeful work. As an international speaker and consultant, he has shared transformational ideas about leadership and trust with people from over 100 countries. His clients include Procter & Gamble, Boeing, the Defense Finance & Accounting Service, LEGO, the City of Miami Beach, and the US Veterans Administration.

Barry currently serves as the chair of the Storytelling in Organizations special interest group of the National Storytelling Network and continues to bring meaning into play with organizations and leaders. Barry is a key faculty member of the Purpose Project Guild, based in the University of Minnesota's Center for Spirituality and Healing.

Barry and his wife, Lorilee, met in France and now live in Utah with their children. They, too, like pie. Barry's interests outside of work include family activities, music, reading, people development, and the American West.

www.ASliceOfTrust.com